I0479463

Crowd Saving at a Glance

by *Desmond Evan Johnson*

(Includes: The MacBook Plan & Crowd Saving)

www.bmvgmaent.com/publishing/merchandise

Bmvgma Publishing

Copyright© 2023 Desmond Evan Johnson

All rights reserved.

Money Motivation

"Call a crowd, put some cash in your pocket today."

<u>Preface</u>

Crowd Saving at a Glance is a brief introduction to Crowd Saving, which is a financial savings practice written and created by Desmond Evan Johnson. Follow as it transforms from Part 1, "The MacBook Plan, " which is an example of how Crowd Saving works, into Part 2, "Crowd Saving, " which lists a detailed account of Crowd Saving the method, some pros and cons on the practice of Crowd Saving and offers a strong pitch to bankers to be incorporated as a secondary method of savings.

An accumulation of Micro-Financing, CD's(Cash Deposits), Loans, Crowdsourcing and what we know as basic Financial Saving today, Crowd Saving has proven to be a 100% safe, new method of saving that could be of great benefit to almost any bank or money managing institution. Not only is Crowd Saving a benefit to Financial Institutions but also to those who choose to apply this unique style of saving.

Contents

Crowd Saving Defined

Crowd Saving is a deposit backed, target based, financial saving method.

Crowd Savings would be the Account Title of the actual financial account if implemented in banks etc.

Instead of Saving Up or Vertical Saving, Crowd Saving allows an individual to save horizontally, with a crowd. Which means every time you save your crowd saves along with you. You receive the whole amount you are saving for, (your target) whenever you receive your first Crowd Payment. Your sales target is met by saving together or Crowd Saving!

(Part 1.)

The MacBook Plan

by Desmond Evan Johnson

Twelve students, in a student club, need MacBook laptops so that they can use the same programs and synchronize without a flaw. Basic Macs are right around a thousand dollars each. How are 12 freshmen at a Community College supposed to fork over a thousand bucks for a Mac?

Simple;

For the next 12 months each person in the group is going to turn in 100 dollars a month. If we started today December 25th, 2018, (Merry Christmas !!,) the first payment of 100 dollars per student is due. Let's say all 12 members turn in 100 dollars today. Now we have 1200 dollars on the table. The first member will receive a CROWD PAYMENT of 1200 dollars and purchase his/hers MacBook by the end of the day. Next month January 25th, all 12 members will repeat the 100 dollar payment and then the second member will get a 1200 dollar CROWD PAYMENT to pick up his Mac for under 1200 dollars. For the next 10 months the same process will be repeated and by December 25th, 2019 all 12 of the members will have MacBook Laptops.

In short, over a 12-month period, all twelve members will pay 100 dollars a month. Each month one member gets a draw or a CROWD PAYMENT of 1200 dollars to buy a MacBook. Saving a hundred a month is cool but if you need 1200 dollars today, this might be the plan for you.

This method can also be applied to vacation, employee and family savings. The amount of money paid monthly by each member and the 12-month period, can be increased or decreased, depending on the need for the money. Car and house down payments, vacations, Christmas money, rent, etc.

Furthered;

Picture swimming in a pool of savers, all in and out of 6, 12, and 18-month, Crowd Saving Plans. A very old practice, the phrase A-Sue is what Crowd Saving was called in the Caribbean versus being called, "Tanda," by some Mexican Americans or " In The Pot," a man from Sri Lanka said. As termed by the creator of The Lifetime Student Foundation and transformed into a more legal, safe practice, Crowd Saving has been used in some countries for centuries as an alternative to banking and sometimes just for an additional savings money on top of banking.

The creation of a Crowd Savings Account would secure the money being paid by each saver and help to create a more legal and safe financial savings practice.

Banks or Money managers would of course benefit from holding the accounts for a small percentage or it can be added as a free service. That would be decided.

<u>Merry Christmas World !!</u>

(Part 2.)

<u>Crowd Saving</u>

by Desmond Evan Johnson

Instead of saving up for something Crowd Saving allows an individual to save horizontally, with a crowd. The MacBook Plan is an example of Crowd Saving.

Twelve students, in a student club, need MacBook laptops so they can use the same programs and synchronize without a flaw. Basic Macs are right around a thousand dollars each. How are 12 freshmen at a Community College supposed to fork over a thousand bucks for a Mac?

Simple;

For the next 12 months each person in the group is going to turn in 100 dollars a month. If we started today December 25th, 2018, (Merry Christmas !!,) the first payment of 100 dollars per student is due. Let's say all 12 members turn in 100 dollars today. Now we have 1200 dollars on the table. The first member will receive a CROWD PAYMENT of 1200 dollars and purchase his Macbook by the end of the day. Next month January 25th, all 12 members will repeat the 100-dollar payment and then the second member will get a 1200-dollar CROWD PAYMENT to pick up his Mac for under 1200. For the next 10 months the same process will be repeated and by December 25th, 2019 all 12 of the members will have MacBook Laptops.

In short, over a 12-month period all twelve members will pay 100 dollars a month. Each month one member gets a draw of 1200 dollars to buy a MacBook. Saving a hundred a month is cool but if you need 1200 dollars today, this might be the plan for you.

This method can also be applied to vacation, employee and family savings. The amount of money paid monthly by each member and the 12-month period can be increased or decreased depending on the need for the money. Car and house down payments, vacations, Christmas money, rent, etc.

Furthered;

Picture swimming in a pool of savers, all in and out of 6, 12, and 18-month Crowd Savings plans?

A very old practice, the phrase pronounced either A-Su or A-Sa is what Crowd Saving was called in the Bahamas. As termed by the creator of The Lifetime Student Foundation and transformed into a more legal and safe practice, Crowd Saving has been used in some countries for centuries as an alternative to banking and sometimes just for additional savings money on top of banking.

The creation of a Crowd Savings Account would secure the Money being paid by each saver and help to create a more legal and safe financial savings practice.

Banks or Money managers would of course benefit from holding the accounts for a small percentage or it can be added as a free service. That would be decided.

Crowd Saving - Based on The MacBook Plan, the following crowd saving plans can get you the total sums;

$100 on a 12-month crowd saving plan with 12 people will get you $1200 today.

$200 on a 12-month crowd saving plan with 12 people will get you $2400 today.

$300 on a 12-month crowd saving plan with 12 people will get you $3600 today.

$400 on a 12-month crowd saving plan with 12 people will get you $4800 today.

$500 on a 12-month crowd saving plan with 12 people will get you $6000 today.

Etc…

And so forth;

$5000 on a 12-month crowd saving plan with 12 people will get you $60,000 today. Just think if you had twelve individuals or groups paying $5000 a month, every month one group gets $60,000 to fund just about anything they want. A chain of stores, restaurants, pay commercial rent, inventory, investment money, repair shops etc. Whatever the individual or group decides.

The only question is what happens when someone does not pay their monthly crowd saving payment?

If instituted in financial institutions such as banks, the best way to suffice for those who do not pay would be to keep the emphasis on savings and only allow those to crowd save if they;

1.   Have an equal amount in savings to cover whatever the amount the crowd saving term is for.

That is, if it's 12 people crowding for $1200 on a 12-month crowd saving term, each saver would have to have an equal amount or more in their savings account to cover the full amount, for the full 6, 12, or 18-month Crowd Saving Term.

The $1200 can be transferred from your savings or checking account to create the <u>Crowd Savings Account</u> and is now the beginning balance in your <u>Crowd Savings Account</u>. So now, if a person misses a $100 payment, the $100 payment will automatically be deducted from the $1200 now being held in your <u>Crowd Savings Account</u>. The $1200 dollars being held guarantees that everyone in the crowd can pay and should be held until the <u>6, 12 or 18 month Crowd Saving Term is complete.</u>

Again, worse case and a saver can't pay one month, the money deducted from savings is still savings money so it's not loss, it's just another savings option you are paying off.

The best part is that all 12 months are covered so that there will be no problems with monthly payments by those in a crowd.

Also, at the end of every Crowd Saving Term, be it 6, 12 or 18 months etc, the $1200 deposit to begin your <u>Crowd Savings Account Balance</u> is released to your <u>Savings</u> account or added to your <u>Crowd Savings Account Balance</u>. (That would be decided)

- If you pay your Crowd Savings fee of $100 every month then you get the full amount of $1200.

- If you don't pay any of your Crowd Saving Fees, of $100 a month for 12 months, then every month $100 would have been deducted from the $1200 being held, so you would get $0.

- Either way, there 's no loss.

Now your <u>Crowd Saving Balance</u> consists of the $1200 you started with on top of whatever your monthly <u>Crowd Savings Account Payment</u> is or what's left of it if you spent some of it.

One Hundred percent safe and ready to be implemented in most financial institutions.

Now our pool of swimmers has increased from 12 to 12 million or potentially billions of savers all in and out of 6, 12 and 18-month, <u>Crowd Saving Plans</u>.

Amazing !!

Or

2.   Bring Your Own Crowd. Which in short means bring your own savers and crowd save with those you have selected to do so with, which is also the way it's done now without a bank involved or a proper safety net. Not as safe as the system in plan 1, it would allow for savers to just make payments on their own, on the selected payment date by the crowd. I would suggest that crowd savers keep the sums low so the amount owed is not too much for a saver to afford.

Hopefully Crowd Saving will be added to your local financial institutions as a savings service soon. Imagine signing into your bank account, clicking on your Savings Account and seeing an option to Crowd Save. Until then, there is a little math for you to work with my fellow scholars.

Money Motivation 2

Figure 2.   (By Desmond Evan Johnson/Bmvgma Photos/2020/"Outside 2nd Street Clothing"/The Camp, Costa mesa, Ca 92626)

"Call a crowd. Put some cash in your pocket today."

Money Motivation

"Call a crowd, put some cash in your pocket today."

www.ingramcontent.com/pod-product-compliance
Lightning Source LLC
Chambersburg PA
CBHW081420220526

45467CB00009B/2761